Jenny Penny is eight years old. Her full name is
Genevieve Penelope Van Holt, but everyone just
calls her Jenny Penny.

She lives in a big old house. Behind the house is a
big field with a big apple tree.

Jenny Penny loves animals.

She has a pet cat called Tiger,
a hamster called Spot, and a
goldfish called Beluga.

Whenever she got the chance, she would go
out behind her house, exploring for animals.

She held up her magnifying glass and saw a
grasshopper. It looked like a tiny kangaroo.
She was very excited.

5

She ran home to her mother.
"Mom! Mom! I found a tiny kangaroo!" She said.

Her mother explained that it was just a
grasshopper, but Jenny Penny was still excited.
She had found a grasshopper!

ne day, Jenny Penny was exploring the field behind
er house.

ne was on her hands and knees, looking for animals.

Suddenly, she bumped into something big.
Something very, very big.

Jenny Penny stood up to look and see what
the big thing was.

It was an elephant! A real live elephant!

This time, Jenny Penny was sure what she had seen. It was a real elephant!

Jenny Penny was very surprised.
Why was there a real live elephant in her
back yard?
And why was he standing by her apple tree?

8

Jenny Penny ran home to her mother.

"Mom! Mom! I found an elephant in our
back yard. Can I keep it? Huh?"
Jenny Penny asked.

"An elephant?" Asked her mother.
"Are you sure, Jenny Penny?"

Jenny Penny jumped up and down.
"Yes! And it's big, and it's eating
the apples on our apple tree.
Come and see."

"Come and see." Jenny Penny said.
"I'll show you the elephant in our yard."

She took her mother's hand and led her
mother out to the field with the apple tree.

Jenny Penny and her mother went out
to the field. Jenny Penny's mother saw the
elephant. She screamed when she saw it.

"Jenny Penny, this is a real elephant."
Her mother said.

"Yes, it's a real elephant." Said Jenny Penny.
"Can I keep him, mom? I really like him."

Her mother shook her head.
"I don't understand how he got here,
Jenny Penny." She said.

"But, he likes me, mom." Jenny Penny said.
"Can I keep him, huh?
I'll take very good care of him, really I will."

The elephant took Jenny Penny's hat
away from her.
That made Jenny Penny laugh.
"See?" She said. "He likes me."

A little while later, Jenny Penny's father came home.
"Dad!" Said Jenny Penny.
"Guess what I found? An elephant. A real live
elephant eating apples in our back yard."

"An elephant, you say?" Asked her father.
"Yes." Said her mother.
"Come and see."

Jenny Penny, her father and mother all went
out to the field to see the elephant.
Her father was surprised to see the elephant there.
"Well, this is interesting." He said.
"Do you think he escaped from a circus?"
"Let's find out. "He said.

nny Penny's father went into the house and called
e police.
Iello." He said. "Do you know if anyone is looking
r an elephant?" He asked.

Vhy? Did you find an elephant?" The police officer
ked.
Yes, we did." Jenny Penny's father said.

Jenny Penny's father explained that there was an elephant in their back yard, and he was eating their apples.
He explained how Jenny Penny had found the elephant and that he was friendly.

The police offier said "Don't worry, we'll come right over."

Very soon after that, a police officer came to speak
with Jenny Penny's father.
"I understand you found an elephant." He said.

"Yes." Said Jenny Penny.
"And he's eating our apples in the back yard."

The police officer went out to the apple tree.
The elephant was sleeping under the tree.
"You have an elephant in your yard." He said.
"This is very unusual, I must say."
He went out to his car and talked on the police
radio, then he came right back.

e police officer came back and spoke to Jenny Penny
d her mother and father.

 found out where the elephant belongs." He said.

Ie was on his way to a zoo, but the truck he was in
pped and he wandered out."

nny Penny was sad that she couldn't keep the elephant.

"I know you are sad." Jenny Penny's father said. "But you can't keep the elephant. You would have to feed him and give him water and exercise every day. He belongs with the other elephants."

Jenny Penny was sad, but she knew her father was right. The elephant belonged with his family.

he police officer called the zoo, and a man from the zoo
ame. He sat beside Jenny Penny.
Hello." He said. "I am one of the zookeepers. I see you
ave taken very good care of our little elephant.
'here did you find him?"

Jenny Penny looked up at the man.
"He was here, eating our apples." She said.

"I see." Said the man.
"We have to take him home to his mother, though.
Would you like to come with us to the zoo?"
"Yes, please!" Said Jenny Penny.

Jenny Penny, her father and the
zookeeper sat in the truck as they all
drove the elephant to the zoo.

Jenny Penny was very excited.
She enjoyed going to the zoo, and she
went there every chance she could go.

When they got to the zoo, the zookeeper stopped the truck beside a big field, which had trees and another elephant.

This elephant was much bigger than Jenny Penny's elephant.

As soon as it saw Jenny Penny's elephant it made a loud trumpet noise.

The zookeeper opened a gate and Jenny
Penny's elephant ran to the bigger elephant.
The bigger elephant wrapped its trunk
around Jenny Penny's elephant.
"There." Said the zookeeper.
"Now he's back with his mother."

Both elephants walked away, toward
some big trees in the field. Jenny Penny
was sad.
"But I really wanted to keep him."
Jenny Penny said.

You can still help us take care of him."
the zookeeper said.
You can come to the zoo any time you like.
You are now an official junior zookeeper."
He put his hat on Jenny Penny's head.

Yay!" She said. "Now I can visit my elephant
any time I want! Yay!"

"Something else." The zookeeper said.
"Your elephant doesn't have a name yet.
Can you think of a name for your elephant?"

Jenny Penny smiled. "I can call him Apple."
She said.

The zookeeper laughed. "That's a very good
name, Jenny Penny. He is now Apple."

lmost every weekend, Jenny Penny would visit
he zoo. She would wear her hat that said 'zoo'
nd Apple the elephant would eat the apples
enny Penny gave him.

'eople would come to see Apple the elephant,
nd Jenny Penny would say:
'Hello, everybody. My name is Jenny Penny,
nd this is my friend, Apple the elephant."
he was very happy. Apple would trumpet with
is trunk. He was happy too.

THE END

This book is dedicated to the people who are important to us.

Our children, grandchildren and especially to my infinitely tolerant wife Alison.

My deepest thanks as well to Hannah Bricknell, whose illustrations bring Jenny Penny to life.

H.B.ORIGINALS

www.ingramcontent.com/pod-product-compliance
Lightning Source LLC
Chambersburg PA
CBHW071259310326
41914CB00109B/706